SPACE!

SATURN

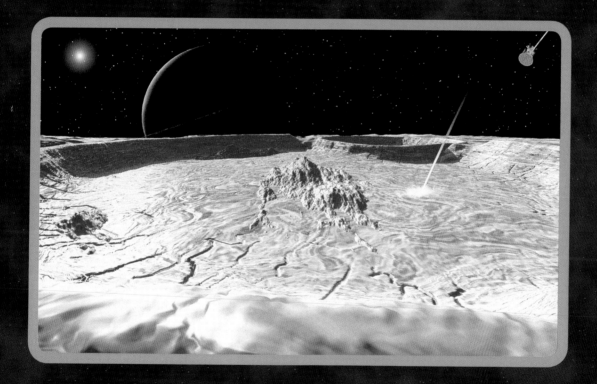

TERRY ALLAN HICKS

 **Marshall Cavendish**
Benchmark
New York

Marshall Cavendish Benchmark
99 White Plains Road
Tarrytown, New York 10591
www.marshallcavendish.us

Library of Congress Cataloging-in-Publication Data
Hicks, Terry Allan.
   Saturn / by Terry Allan Hicks.
       p. cm. -- (Space!)
   Summary: "Describes Saturn, including its history, its composition, and its role in the
solar system"--Provided by publisher.
   Includes bibliographical references and index.
   ISBN 978-07614-4249-3
   1. Saturn (Planet)--Juvenile literature. I. Title.
   QB671.H53 2010
   523.46--dc22
   2008037453

Editor: Karen Ang
Publisher: Michelle Bisson
Art Director: Anahid Hamparian
Series Design by Daniel Roode
Production by nSight, Inc.

Front cover: A computer illustration of Saturn
Title page: The surface of Rhea, one of Saturn's moons
Photo research by Candlepants Incorporated
Front cover: Brand X / Super Stock
The photographs in this book are used by permission and through the courtesy of:
Super Stock: Pixtal, 1, 12; Digital Vision Ltd., 9, 39, 58. Corbis: 4, 5, 30, 32, 33; NASA/Roger
Ressmeyer, 14; STScI/NASA, 35. Art Resource, NY: Réunion des Musées Nationaux, 7; Erich
Lessing, 21. Getty Images: Kevin Kelley, 10. Photo Researchers Inc.: Mark Garlick, 15, 34;
The Bridgeman Art Library, 20; Mary Evans, 23; 25. AP Images: NASA, 18, 19; European
Space Agency/ESOC, 50. The Image Works: World History / Topham, 27; Oxford Science
Archive / Heritage-Images, 24. NASA: Ames Research Center, 29; JPL/Space Science
Institute, 36, 40, 41, 42, 43, 44, 45, 46, 47, 48, 55; JPL/JHUAPL, 51; Craig Attebery, 53; ESA/
JPL/University of Arizona, 54. Illustration on page 17 by Mapping Specialists © Marshall
Cavendish Corporation.
Printed in Malaysia
123456

CONTENTS

1

THE RINGED PLANET

On July 1, 2004, a spacecraft approached the planet Saturn, a mysterious **celestial** object that has fascinated people on Earth for centuries. The unmanned vehicle, named *Cassini-Huygens,* had been launched from the space center at Cape Canaveral, Florida, almost seven years earlier. As the spacecraft neared the planet, it slowed itself down and allowed Saturn's **gravity** to capture it. For at least the next four years, *Cassini-Huygens* would circle—or **orbit**—Saturn, while the spacecraft's highly sensitive instruments sent back valuable new information.

Saturn is the sixth planet from the Sun and is the second-largest planet in the Solar System. Saturn has a diameter of 74,900 miles (121,000 kilometers) and is so big that about 760 planets the size of Earth could fit inside it. This yellowish-brown planet is marked by shifting horizontal bands of color and is surrounded by dozens of **moons**.

Because of its many visible rings, Saturn is one of the most recognizable planets in our Solar System.

But what truly sets Saturn apart from the other planets in the Solar System is not its size or its moons, but the amazing system of rings that surround it. Thousands of multicolored bands circle the planet at its **equator**, shimmering with reflected light from the Sun. Other planets have rings, but none are as dazzling as Saturn's. Ever since they were first discovered, almost exactly four centuries ago, **astronomers** have been struggling to understand Saturn's rings—what they are and how they were created.

ANCIENT EYES ON SATURN

People on Earth have been aware of Saturn's existence since ancient times. Anyone carefully watching the night sky could see it for most of the year, just as we can today. To the naked eye, it would have appeared as a yellowish spot, a little larger and a little brighter than most of the thousands of stars that could be seen on any cloudless night. At times, it would actually have been the brightest spot in the night sky. But to early astronomers, there was little about this heavenly body to make it seem different from all the rest—except for the unusual way it acted.

Ancient astronomers, scientists, and religious leaders in places as far apart as Babylon and China, Egypt and India, knew that the Sun, Moon, and stars all seemed to move across the sky.

An artifact from around 400 BCE to 350 BCE shows astronomical observations made by Eudoxus of Cnidus, an ancient Greek astronomer.

Most of these early sky watchers mistakenly believed that all of the bodies in the heavens circled Earth. Scientists did not begin to realize that this Earth-centered view of the heavens was wrong until about five hundred years ago. The early observers watched the celestial objects closely, trying to follow and predict their movements. The sky watchers noticed that a very few of these objects—including the one we know today as Saturn—did not move the same way as the rest. These "stars" appeared to be in different **constellations**, or groups of stars, at different times. They also seemed to grow brighter or dimmer at different times. It was clear that they were somehow different from the other stars. But many centuries passed before people came to understand that these unusual objects were not stars at all, but planets orbiting the Sun, the same way Earth does.

Saturn is now perhaps the best-loved planet of all, a favorite for astronomers to watch and for schoolchildren to draw. But it was not always a favorite because it was not easy to see. Until strong telescopes were invented, no one even knew about its now-famous rings.

ACROSS THE UNIVERSE

To anyone staring up at the sky, the size of the **universe** seems absolutely overwhelming. In fact, the universe is even larger than most of us realize—perhaps even larger than we can imagine. The known, or visible, universe—the part we can "see" with telescopes and other types of instruments—is about 28 billion **light-years** from one side to the other. No one can even guess at the size of the parts of the universe that we cannot see. Many astronomers, **physicists**, and other scientists who study space believe that as huge as the universe is, it may still be expanding.

LIGHT-YEARS

The distances in the universe are so great that a special unit, the light-year, was created to measure them. Most scientists believe that nothing will ever be able to travel faster than the speed of light, which moves through empty space at a rate of about 186,282 miles (299,792 km) per second. A light-year is the distance—about 5.9 trillion miles (9.5 trillion km)—that light travels in a year.

It is possible that the universe is actually infinite, with no beginning and no end.

The most important bodies in the universe are the stars, huge balls of flaming gas spinning in space. There are so many stars that so far, no one has even come close to being able to count them. About eight thousand stars are visible from Earth without a telescope, though only about half of them can be seen from any one point at any one time.

There are billions of stars in the universe, though only some are visible to us from Earth.

Some astronomers estimate that there may be 70 sextillion—that is the number seven, followed by twenty-two zeros—stars in the known universe alone.

Most stars are part of **galaxies**, which are enormous, slowly revolving clusters of stars, gases, dust particles, and other matter that are scattered throughout the universe. There are hundreds of millions of galaxies in the known universe, and a single galaxy may have trillions of stars. The galaxy we live in, which is known as the Milky Way, is hardly the largest galaxy in the universe, but it, too, contains hundreds of billions of stars. One of those stars is our Sun—the center of the Solar System.

An image from the Hubble Space Telescope shows details of the M100 galaxy. Like the Milky Way, M100 is called a spiral galaxy because of its shape.

EARTH'S NEIGHBORHOOD

The Solar System is made up of the Sun and all the many objects that are held in place by its massive gravitational force. (The Solar System is named for the Sun. Sol is another name for the Sun, and *solar* means "of the Sun.") There are billions of objects orbiting the Sun, some of them huge, many of them not much larger than specks of dust. They include the eight inner, or **terrestrial**, planets (Mercury, Venus, Earth, and Mars) and the four outer or gas planets (Jupiter, Saturn, Uranus, and Neptune). But many other objects circle the Sun, including at least five **dwarf planets**—one of them, Pluto, was considered a regular planet until recently—and at least 170 moons, as well as **comets**, **asteroids**, and many other smaller bodies.

The Sun

The Sun is not the biggest star in the sky, or the brightest. The largest star that astronomers have identified so far, which is called VY Canis Majoris, is more than two thousand times the size of the Sun. The brightest star, the Pistol Star, may give off almost 2 million times as much light, producing more energy in a single minute than the Sun does in an entire year. Despite their size and brightness, neither of these stars can be seen from Earth without special instruments because they are extremely far away and our view of them is blocked by dust clouds in space.

11

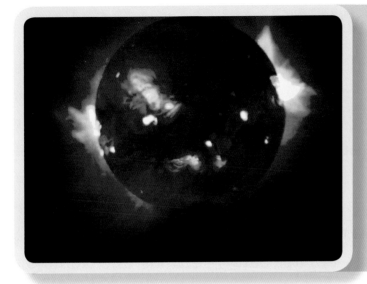

Scientists predict that the Sun will run out of hydrogen and burn out in about 4.5 billion years. Until then, this intense star will continue to be the central point in our Solar System.

Even if the Sun is not the biggest or brightest, it is the most important star for the people and other living things here on Earth. This is because it is the one closest to us. The Sun is roughly 93 million miles (150 million km) away from our planet. The Sun's light takes about eight minutes to travel to Earth. The light from the next-closest star, Alpha Centauri, takes a little more than four years to reach us. Some stars that have recently been discovered in distant galaxies are more than a billion light-years away from Earth.

The Sun is also the biggest and most powerful object in Earth's neighborhood. It is six hundred times larger than everything else in the Solar System combined. It is also the most important energy source in the Solar System, producing incredible amounts of light and heat. The Sun also has more than 99 percent of all the **mass** in the Solar System. This incredible amount of mass creates the gravitational force that keeps everything else in the Solar System orbiting around the Sun.

The Solar System began to come into existence about 4.5 billion years ago. Scientists believe that this happened when a cloud of hydrogen and other gases and dust at the edge of the Milky Way began to come together. Nobody knows exactly why this happened, but it may have been the result of the explosion of a nearby star. Whatever the cause, the powerful gravity at the center of the cloud began to pull the gases and dust particles together. They became more tightly packed, and hotter, until an enormous explosion occurred, creating a star—the star we know today as our Sun.

The Birth of the Planets

The force of the explosion was felt far beyond the Sun. It sent gas and dust particles flying into space. The Sun's gravity caused these particles to form into a ring that revolved around it, and their own gravity caused them to collide with one another. Slowly, over a period of at least 100,000 years, groups of particles began to combine into small bodies called planetesimals. These eventually became all the objects—including the planets—that now orbit around the Sun.

The Sun's heat, or rather the lack of it, is the main reason the planets farthest away from the center of the Solar System—such as Saturn—are also the biggest. The planets closest to the Sun—Earth, Mars, Mercury, and Venus—were exposed to intense heat, which made it difficult or impossible for ice to form. The result was that these planets were made up mostly of dust particles that, as they grew and developed more and more gravity, were forced together, forming into metallic rock.

Farther away from the Sun's heat, planets formed differently. In these colder regions, a planet's rocky core could attract not only dust particles, but also ice and gases. The four planets that were created there attracted more matter, so they became larger and acquired more mass. More mass meant that the planets' gravity increased and they acquired even more matter and mass. These

Planetesimals pick up matter as they move through space and collide with other planetesimals and celestial bodies.

A huge expanse of space lies between the inner and outer planets, between the paths of Mars's and Jupiter's orbits. A planet could not be created in this area, 150 to 370 million miles (241 to 595 million km) from the Sun, because it would have been torn apart by the huge gravitational force of Jupiter. But billions of irregularly shaped pieces of rock called asteroids—some large, but most less than 150 miles (241 km) in diameter—orbit the Sun in this zone. Most of the asteroids in the Solar System are found in this area, which is known as the asteroid belt, but the very largest asteroids are found farther away from the Sun, on the edge of the Solar System.

outer planets continued growing for millions of years longer than the inner planets. The outer planets—Jupiter, Saturn, Uranus, and Neptune—became the gas giants we know today.

The gas giants are hostile, unwelcoming places, and Saturn is no exception. It is extremely unlikely that any human being will ever set foot on the surface of the ringed planet. For one thing, there really is no surface, or at least no solid matter, for anyone to stand on. Saturn's "surface" is mostly gas, with some liquid, and some strange areas that are like gas in some ways and like liquid in others. The planet's atmosphere is made up mostly of hydrogen and helium, which humans cannot breathe. Saturn is also bitterly cold, with average temperatures far lower than even the coldest places on Earth. Saturn's surface is also swept by powerful winds and violent storms.

Even so, human beings are still fascinated by Saturn. This is why astronomers have been watching it since even before they knew it was a planet. It is why we have spent many years and many billions of dollars building advanced spacecraft to explore Saturn. It sometimes seems that the more we learn about Saturn, the more questions we have. And we cannot help but wonder what other secrets this ring-circled, storm-racked, gas-shrouded giant may still be hiding.

Of the eight main planets in our solar system, the four closest to the Sun—Mercury, Venus, Earth, and Mars—are the terrestrial, or land, planets. Jupiter, Saturn, Uranus, and Neptune are considered gas giants. Pluto, which was once considered a main planet alongside the others, is now known as a dwarf planet.

2

SATURN THROUGH THE AGES

It is impossible to say who first noticed Saturn in the night sky, but it was certainly a very long time ago. People have likely been aware of Saturn's existence since prehistoric times. The earliest known writing about the planet comes from the Assyrians, a people who lived in ancient Mesopotamia (modern-day Iraq). They were skilled astronomers who created a calendar based on the movements of the stars and other celestial objects, possibly as early as 3000 BCE An Assyrian tablet dating from about 700 BCE describes a "sparkle" in the heavens. The Assyrians named it the Star of Ninib, after one of their most important gods.

An image of Saturn taken by *Voyager 2* in 1981 shows the planet's true colors and three of its many moons.

This ancient Babylonian tablet displays early astronomers' observations of the movement of the stars and planets.

Many other ancient peoples were aware that some of the "stars" in the sky did not act the way other stars did. Five of these celestial objects, in particular, changed their position and brightness over time, seeming to follow the paths of the Sun and the moon closely. Three centuries after the Assyrians first mentioned the Star of Ninib, the Greeks called these curious bodies *planetes*, or "wanderers," which is the source of the English word *planet*.

The Greeks, like the Assyrians and many other people, named the celestial objects they saw after their gods and other figures from mythology. They named the most distant of the *planetes* for Kronos, the father of Zeus, the most important of the Greek gods. The Romans, whose mythology was similar to the Greeks', knew Kronos by a different name. They called him, and the planet, Saturnus, which is where we get the modern-day name Saturn.

Many ancient peoples believed that celestial objects played an important role in affairs on Earth. There is some truth to this, because gravitational and other forces affect many aspects of life on our planet, from the ocean tides to the seasons to the weather. For reasons we do not entirely understand, many of these peoples traditionally associated the planet we know as Saturn with farming. Saturnus was the Roman god of agriculture, among other things. The scientific symbol for Saturn represents a sickle, the harvesting tool the god was often shown carrying.

The Roman god Saturn is depicted on this fourth-century stone carving.

BEGINNING TO SEE SATURN CLEARLY

By the sixteenth century, a few astronomers and other scientists were beginning to understand that the traditional view of the heavens—that all the objects in the sky moved around the earth—was wrong. Nicolaus Copernicus, a Polish astronomer, developed a **heliocentric**, or Sun-centered view of the Solar System. In writings published in 1543, he claimed that all the planets, including Earth, actually orbited the Sun. A few years later, a young German scientist named Johannes Kepler discovered that the planets' orbits were not perfectly circular. This meant that their distance from Earth changed, which helped to explain why they sometimes seemed brighter than at other times. Their distance from the Sun also changed, and Kepler found that the closer an object was to the Sun, the faster it moved through space. Kepler's ideas were very important to the growing understanding of Saturn and its rings.

The first person to observe Saturn through a telescope was a great Italian astronomer, Galileo Galilei, who had been greatly influenced by these new ideas. His telescope was a very early model that magnified objects to only twenty times their actual size, so he could not see the planet very clearly. But what he did see, beginning in 1610, amazed him. That year, he wrote, "I have discovered a most extraordinary marvel . . . the planet Saturn is not one alone, but is composed of three, which almost touch one another." He did not know it, but what he thought were two extra planets were actually Saturn's rings. As he kept watching, he saw that Saturn seemed to change. Two years after his first observations, he found he could no longer see the two extra planets at all. But four years later, in 1616, something else that he described as looking like "handles" had mysteriously appeared.

Using his handmade telescope, Galileo was able to observe Saturn, its rings, and one of its moons, though he did not realize he was seeing a moon and rings.

SATURN

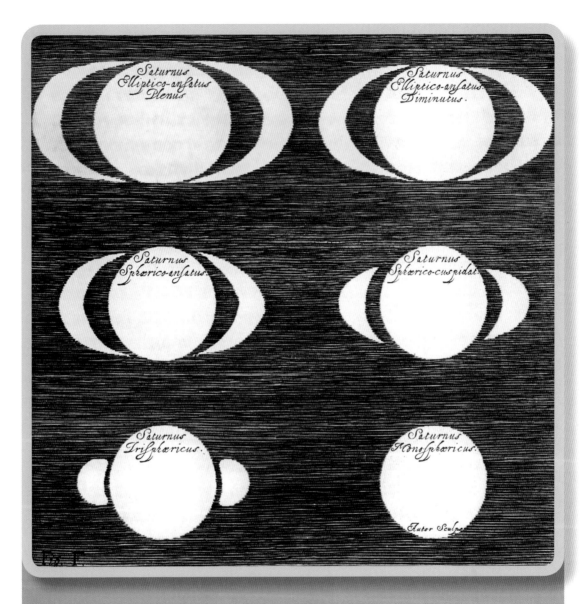

These drawings were created in 1656 by Johannes Hevelius, a German astronomer who observed the different appearances of Saturn. At the time, he did not realize that the strange shapes he was seeing next to Saturn were its rings.

UNDERSTANDING THE RINGS

It was not until forty-five years after Galileo's discovery that it became clear what Saturn's strange, seemingly ever-changing shape really meant. A Dutch mathematician, physicist, and astronomer named Christiaan Huygens, had a telescope much stronger than Galileo's. With that telescope, he discovered a moon orbiting Saturn—the huge one that later came to be called Titan. The following year, he realized that what Galileo had seen must have been "a thin, flat ring" surrounding, but not touching, the planet. The reason it had looked so different to Galileo at different times was that he had observed the planet at different angles and different points in its orbit. When Saturn was tipped toward Earth, what Galileo saw looked like extra planets or

Christiaan Huygens was the first to realize that Saturn was a ringed planet, but his assumption that there was only one ring was incorrect.

the handles of a cup, depending on the angle. When the planet was positioned so that the rings were horizontal in relation to Earth, they seemed to have disappeared.

Huygens was right about Saturn being a ringed planet, but he was wrong about some other things. He believed there was just one ring, several thousand miles thick, made of solid rock. One important Saturn-watcher who disagreed with him was an Italian-French astronomer named Giovanni Domenico (or Jean Dominique) Cassini. Cassini made many important discoveries about Saturn, including the first sightings of four of the planet's moons—Dione, Iapetus, Rhea, and Tethys. Looking through the powerful telescope at the new Paris **Observatory** in 1675, Cassini saw that there was a space in Saturn's ring, which suggested that it was actually two rings. That space is known to this day as the Cassini Division. Cassini believed the rings were made up of many different particles, rather than solid matter. It took more than two hundred years before this was finally settled.

In the decades that followed, many more discoveries were made about Saturn, but none of them were quite as dramatic as Huygens's and Cassini's breakthroughs. More rings were discovered (and another space between rings, known as the Encke Division) and more moons. Then, in the late nineteenth century, the question of whether Saturn's rings were solid was answered once and for all.

Cassini used the strong telescopes at the Paris Observatory in France to identify four more moons of Saturn and to closely observe the planet's multiple rings.

Astronomers had discovered a third, semitransparent ring, closer to the planet's surface than the first two. A Scottish mathematician and physicist, James Clerk Maxwell, suggested that Saturn's rings would have to be made up of different particles, because if they were not, the planet's powerful gravity would pull them toward it and destroy them. He also suggested, drawing on Johannes Kepler's now-centuries-old ideas, that the three known rings would have to revolve at different speeds,

NAMING THE RINGS

Saturn and its moons, like many other celestial objects, have colorful names taken from the mythologies of the Greeks, the Romans, and other ancient peoples, but its rings do not. The seven major rings that are clearly separate have simply been given letters—A, B, C, D, E, F, and G—that reflect the order in which they were discovered. The A and B rings were first observed by Galileo in 1610, though he did not know what he was looking at. It was not until 370 years later, in 1980, that the G ring was identified.

the one closest to the planet moving the fastest. In 1895, an American astronomer, James Keeler, proved Maxwell—and Huygens—right. He used an instrument called a spectroscope to measure the speed at which the rings revolved, and discovered that the "inside" ring did indeed move faster than the others.

Scientists continued to try to understand how these strange rings could have been created. A nineteenth-century French astronomer, Edouard Roche, developed a theory that the rings might have resulted when a moon or other large celestial object approached Saturn and was shattered by the planet's gravitational force. This would have left rock and other particles floating in space, held there forever by Saturn's gravity. Another theory is that the rings are simply made up of particles left over from the creation of the planet itself.

A STEP INTO SPACE

The next great step forward in mankind's understanding of Saturn did not come until the second half of the twentieth century, when powerful rockets began to make space travel possible. The first spacecraft to come close to Saturn, in 1979, was *Pioneer 11,* an unmanned probe that the National Aeronautics and Space Administration (NASA) had sent to study Jupiter. *Pioneer 11* came to within 13,000 miles (21,000 km) of Saturn and sent back the best photographs that had ever been taken

This image taken by *Pioneer II* gave astronomers a nice view of Saturn, its rings, and Titan (upper left).

An illustration shows the path that *Voyager 2* took as it passed by Saturn.

of the ringed planet. (The spacecraft discovered the previously unknown F ring and identified another moon, Epimetheus.) *Pioneer 11*'s instruments showed that Saturn has a magnetic field, which proved that the planet's core is made of metallic rock.

The following year, two more unmanned NASA probes, *Voyager 1* and *Voyager 2*, began a long-planned visit to the outer planets. They had been designed to visit all four of the gas giants, and NASA had sent two of them, just in case one did not complete its mission. *Voyager 1* reached Saturn late in 1980, coming much closer to the planet than *Pioneer 11* had. The probe sent back the first high-resolution images of Saturn, discovered three more moons and the G ring, and found helium in the planet's atmosphere. *Voyager 1* also passed close enough to Titan that scientists learned that the moon has an atmosphere—the only moon in the Solar System known to have one. Unfortunately, the clouds of gas in the atmosphere made it impossible to take pictures of the moon's surface. The companion probe, *Voyager 2,* took even more dazzling pictures of the planet.

In the years that followed, other excellent photographic images of Saturn were received, from the Hubble Space Telescope, which orbits Earth. Then, in 1997, *Cassini-Huygens*—named for the great seventeenth-century astronomers who had made so many important discoveries about Saturn—was launched. *Cassini-Huygens* was very different from *Pioneer* and *Voyager.* Those spacecraft had been used to investigate many other celestial objects, but *Cassini-Huygens* was intended to focus entirely on Saturn and its neighborhood. The mission was actually designed in two parts. *Cassini,* an orbiter, would circle around Saturn for four years or more. *Huygens,* a separate probe, would separate from *Cassini* and land on the surface of Titan.

The two spacecraft are carrying an incredible collection of sensitive instruments. They also carry advanced cameras that have sent back breathtaking high-resolution images of Saturn and the surrounding bodies, especially Titan. These pictures, and the measurements taken by *Cassini-Huygens*'s other instruments, have added to our understanding of the ringed planet.

3

A CLOSER LOOK

People's fascination with Saturn has always focused on the rings and, to a lesser extent, on the planet's moons. But as the scientists who study the planet learn more about Saturn, they are coming to realize that what is inside the planet is every bit as interesting as what is outside.

A PLANET FROM THE INSIDE OUT

The central core of this gas giant is a sphere of solid rock. It is small compared to the planet as a whole, though it may actually

Multiple images taken by *Voyager I* were used to create this picture of Saturn and some of its moons.

be as large as all of Earth. The next layer is an inner **mantle** of liquid hydrogen. Then there is an outer mantle, also made of hydrogen, which is liquid deeper down and becomes gas closer to the surface. The transition from liquid to gas makes it very difficult to tell where Saturn's surface begins and ends. There is actually a part of the surface, called the supercritical area, where the hydrogen that makes up both surface and atmosphere has some characteristics of a liquid and some of a gas.

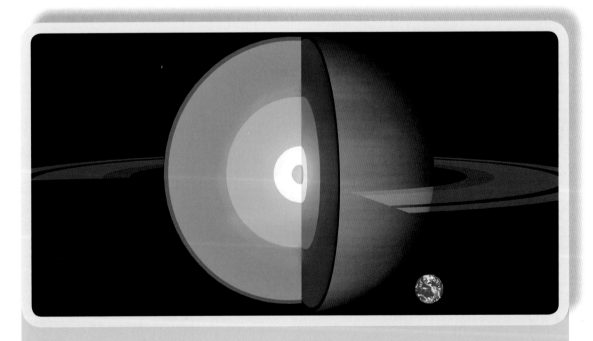

Scientists think that Saturn is made of layers of rock and liquid and gaseous hydrogen. Earth has been included in this image (bottom right) to show how small it is compared to Saturn. Our planet is almost the size of Saturn's core.

SATURN'S MAGNETISM

The Voyager missions discovered that Saturn's core sends out radio waves. Scientists have used these radio waves to determine that the planet's different layers rotate at different speeds. This rotation gives Saturn its magnetic field, which is 1,000 times more powerful than Earth's. The magnetic field wraps the planet, its rings, and its moons in a "charged" area called the magnetosphere.

Saturn's atmosphere—which is made up of 93 percent hydrogen and 6 percent helium, with very small amounts of some other elements—has three separate layers of clouds. The bluish clouds closest to the planet's surface are made up of water, in the form of vapor and ice. Above that is a layer of dark orange clouds of ammonium hydrosulfide crystals. Then comes a layer of white ammonia-crystal clouds, with a pale haze above it. These shifting cloud layers, driven by high winds, are what make the planet's surface look as if it were covered by moving bands of yellow and brown.

An aurora is seen in the atmosphere over Saturn's south pole. Solar particles from the Sun interact with Saturn's magnetic field to create this colorful display.

Weather

The winds on Saturn are breathtaking by Earth standards. They reach speeds of at least 1,118 miles (1,800 km) per hour, with the strongest winds in the areas around the planet's equator.

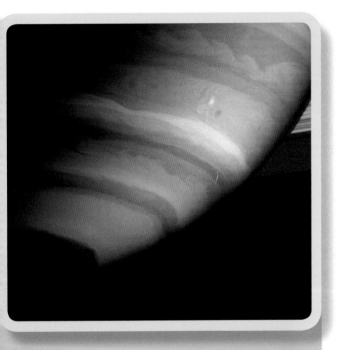

The bright orange swirls are part of the Dragon Storm, which is one of many storms in the planet's southern hemisphere. Because of the fierce weather activity, this part of the planet is often called Storm Alley.

By comparison, the strongest wind ever recorded on Earth was just 231 miles (372 km) per hour. The planet's surface and atmosphere are also affected by sudden, violent storms. One huge storm, known as the Great White Spot, occurs once every time Saturn orbits the Sun and lasts for about a month.

Saturn is extremely cold, with average surface temperatures around -300 degrees Fahrenheit (-185 degrees Celsius). This is not surprising because of the planet's great distance from the Sun's heat and energy. What is surprising is that Saturn actually gives off more heat than it takes in from the Sun. There are many theories that try to explain this. One is that gravity draws matter toward the core of the planet, causing friction and creating heat. Another is that the planet is slowly releasing gas that has been trapped inside it since it was created.

Rotation

Every planet in the Solar System rotates, or spins, on its **axis**. However, Saturn's rotation is unusual. The planet spins very fast—faster than any planet except Jupiter. Earth takes twenty-four hours, or one Earth day, to spin on its axis. Even though Saturn is much larger, its rotation takes only 10 hours and 32 minutes (measured in Earth time) at the equator, and about 30 minutes longer at the poles. This difference in rotation speeds is responsible for another of Saturn's distinctive features: its "flattened" shape. The planet is not a perfect sphere, but is visibly "pushed out" along the equator. All rotating bodies, including Earth, are like this, but the distortion of Saturn's shape is more distinct than with any other planet in the Solar System.

There are other things about Saturn that are highly unusual. Despite its huge size, it has surprisingly little mass and density. It is actually the least dense of all the planets, which makes it extremely light—lighter than water, in fact. The entire planet could actually float in a bucket of water, if someone could find a bucket big enough.

COMPARING SATURN AND EARTH

	SATURN	EARTH
DISTANCE FROM THE SUN	839 million miles (1.3 billion km)	93 million miles (150 million km)
DIAMETER	74,900 miles (121,000 km)	7,926 miles (12,756 km)
AVERAGE SURFACE TEMPERATURE	-300 degrees Fahrenheit (-185 degrees C)	60 degrees Fahrenheit (15 degrees C)
LENGTH OF YEAR	29.5 Earth years	365 days
LENGTH OF DAY	10 hours and 32 minutes	24 hours
NUMBER OF MOONS	61 or more	1
COMPOSITION OF PLANET	Mostly hydrogen (gas and liquid), with a rocky core	Mostly metals and rock
ATMOSPHERE	Mostly hydrogen	Mostly nitrogen and oxygen

UNDERSTANDING THE RINGS

For centuries, Saturn was believed to be the only ringed planet. But in 1979, *Voyager 1* discovered rings around Jupiter. Since then, ring systems have also been found around Uranus and Neptune. Some scientists believe Mars may also have rings. But one thing is certain—no other planet has rings as spectacular as Saturn's.

Saturn's complex ring system begins only about 42,000 miles (67,000 km) above the planet's surface. That is a very small distance, considering Saturn's size. Many of the questions scientists have been asking about Saturn's rings for centuries have now been answered. We know, for example, that the rings are mostly made up of trillions of particles of ice, with some pieces of rock and other matter mixed in. Most of the particles in the rings are small—many as small as bits of dust—while some are as big as a truck or a house.

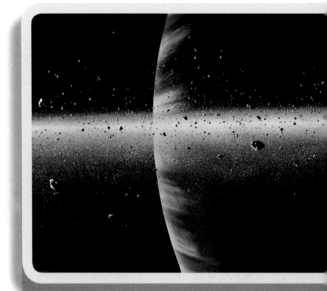

Saturn's rings are not solid strips of material. They are made of billions of particles of varying size, held together by gravity.

These particles make up a huge ring system that is 225,000 miles (362,000 km) wide, from the inside to the outside. But it is not very thick. Scientists have widely varying opinions about this question, but it is clear that in most places the rings are no more than 300 feet (100 meters) from top to bottom. The rings' thinness is what sometimes makes them difficult to see.

The rings are not quite the consistent bands they seem to be at first glance. Each of the seven main rings is made up of thousands, even tens of thousands, of smaller rings. These ringlets do not always follow the ring's shape perfectly. Some are elliptical, rather than circular, and some do not form complete rings around the planet. There are differences among the rings, as well. Because they are made up of trillions of differently shaped particles, they reflect the Sun's light differently, which means there are subtle differences in color and brightness.

Some of Saturn's rings, especially the B ring, have a strange feature that scientists have not yet been able to explain. These are what look like "spokes" in the rings. These dark bands change

Because the ring particles are different sizes, shapes, and material, they all reflect the sunlight differently, creating a colorful glow.

rapidly in location and appearance. The F ring has what looks like braids in it. Scientists believe both of these phenomena might be caused by particles being charged by Saturn's powerful magnetic field, but no one knows for certain what causes them.

The smudge-like darker areas on the lighter-colored rings are the spokes that scientists have observed in some of Saturn's rings.

There is still much that we do not understand about Saturn's rings, but we do know why they circle the planet's equator. That is where Saturn's mass is greatest, so that is where its gravity is strongest. (Some scientists have suggested that the planet's powerful magnetic field may also play a role.) But there is another important, and somewhat surprising, factor helping to keep the rings in place—the planet's many moons.

MANY MOONS

Saturn's most spectacular feature, after its rings, is certainly its moons. Only Jupiter seems to have more moons, and only Jupiter has a moon that is larger than Saturn's largest. (Another name for a moon, or any other body that orbits around a larger one, is a **satellite**.) We do not even know for certain exactly

The close-up image of Phoebe, from *Cassini-Huygens*, shows how the moon resembles an asteroid or comet.

how many moons Saturn has. When the *Cassini-Huygens* mission began in 1997, only eighteen moons had been identified. Today, we know of at least sixty-one moons, and fifty-two of those have been given names.

Most of the moons of Saturn are remarkably regular in their movements. Seven of them are aligned with the planet's equator, just as the rings are. Unlike most moons in the Solar System, they travel in almost perfectly circular orbits and in the same direction. There is one notable exception that fascinates scientists—the little moon called Phoebe. Phoebe is the moon farthest from Saturn, nearly 8 million miles (13 million km) away from the planet. It moves in the opposite direction of the other moons. It also rotates clockwise, while all the other moons, and the planet itself, rotate counterclockwise.

It is not yet clear exactly how Saturn's moons were created, but most of them probably formed at about the same time and in about the same way. The exception is Phoebe, which probably began as a comet or asteroid that was caught by the planet's gravity.

Despite their similarities, there are also great differences among Saturn's moons. Some are huge and some are—by the standards of the Solar System—tiny. The largest, Titan, is 3,200 miles (5,150 km) in diameter, which makes it even larger than the planet Mercury and almost 50 percent larger than Earth's Moon. Yet the smallest of Saturn's moons, which were discovered only recently, are barely 2 miles (3.2 km) wide.

Titan is made up largely of rock, but the other large moons circling Saturn are mostly formed from ice. The moons are different from one another in many other ways, as well. They orbit the planet at very different distances, from as close as 83,015 miles (133,600 km)—well inside the ring system—to as far away as 8 million miles (13 million km). They look very different, too. Some are covered with craters, others have sharp ridges. One, Enceladus, is coated entirely with ice that reflects the Sun's light. This also makes Enceladus the brightest body in the entire Solar System, apart from the Sun.

Saturn's A and F rings are shown here, with Titan (orange) in the background and Epimetheus (white) above.

TITAN

Scientists are really fascinated with Titan, and not just because it is the largest of Saturn's moons. It is also the only moon in the Solar System known to have an atmosphere which, like Earth's, is rich in nitrogen, one of the "building blocks" of life. Many scientists think Titan may be quite similar to the young planet Earth billions of years ago. One of the reasons why the *Cassini-Huygens* mission sent a probe to Titan's surface was to try to learn more about what Earth may have been like in its earliest days.

A colorized image of Minas shows its cratered surface.

Some of Saturn's moons seem to show traces of the violent forces at work in the universe. Minas, for example, has an enormous crater, 80 miles (129 km) across, that covers nearly one-third of the moon's surface. Minas's crater seems to be the result of a destructive collision with some other body. Hyperion appears to be a piece of a larger moon that broke apart at some point in the past. Two small moons, Janus and Epimetheus, may be the two halves of one moon that broke apart when it was struck by a meteorite.

A few of Saturn's moons seem to play a very special role by helping to keep the planet's rings in place. These small moons—which include Atlas, Daphnis, Pan, Pandora, and Prometheus—orbit very close to Saturn's ring system. Two of them orbit inside the rings themselves. Their gravity balances with Saturn's to help hold the particles in the rings in a steady path around the planet.

This entire complex system, like Earth and everything else in the Solar System, revolves around the Sun. Saturn orbits the Sun, taking its rings and its moons with it. But it takes much longer to make

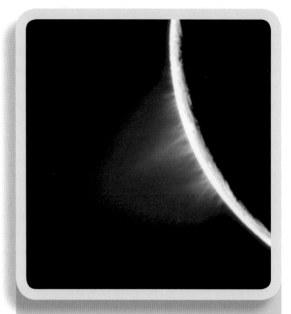

Besides being the brightest moon, the icy Enceladus has ice geysers that shoot out ice, water vapors, and other particles from just below the moon's surface.

a complete orbit than Earth does. It is much farther away from the Sun, so its orbit is much larger, about 5.4 billion miles (8.7 billion km) and moves much more slowly. Earth, moving at about 18.5 miles (30 km) per second, completes an orbit in one year—about 365 days. Saturn revolves around the Sun at only about one-fifth of that speed—6 miles (9.6 km) per second. So a Saturn year takes about 29.5 Earth years.

4

SATURN AND BEYOND

When *Cassini-Huygens* slipped into Saturn's orbit—passing through the gap between the F and G rings—it almost immediately began adding information to what we already knew about the planet. The spacecraft's sensitive, highly advanced instruments and cameras began sending back the most stunning images of the ringed planet that had ever been seen.

A VERY SPECIAL SPACECRAFT

The *Cassini-Huygens* mission is different from any other mission ever launched from Earth, and the spacecraft it uses is different from any other. *Cassini-Huygens* was actually created as two

The specialized equipment on *Cassini-Huygens*, has made it possible for us to see the different colors that Saturn displays.

separate space vehicles, launched into space by a rocket, and carried to Saturn together.

Cassini, which is 22 feet (6.7 m) long and 13.1 feet (4 m) wide and weighed 4,685 pounds (2,215 kilograms) before its fuel was loaded, is an orbiter. It was designed to complete at least seventy orbits of Saturn and many flybys of the planet's rings and moons over a period of four years or more. During these orbits, it would investigate Saturn's atmosphere, interior structure, and magnetosphere, analyze the material in and around the rings, and study the moons, especially Titan, Dione, Iapetus, and Rhea.

Cassini carries twelve highly sophisticated instruments, including two very sensitive cameras, several different types of spectrometers and spectrographs for measuring different types of light and other energy, and a cosmic dust analyzer. The dust analyzer will actually collect particles from the E ring, in the hope of determining whether the rings are made up of the same material as Saturn's moons. This would

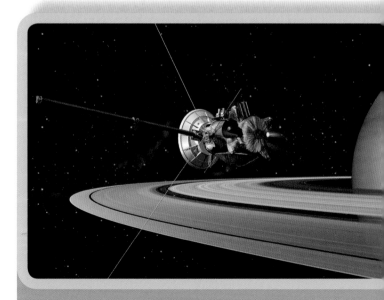

Cassini was designed to orbit Saturn and collect data on the planet's rings, moons, and other features.

The *Cassini-Huygens* mission is an international project. It is a $3.26 billion project that involves NASA, the European Space Agency (ESA), and the Italian Space Agency (ISA). NASA built and controls the *Cassini* orbiter. However, the orbiter's special communications antenna, which is crucial to the mission's success, came from Italy. The ESA built the *Huygens* probe. The information the mission sends back is being analyzed by more than 250 scientists all around the world.

help to prove that the rings were formed by the destruction of earlier moons.

The *Huygens* probe is very different from *Cassini*. It is much smaller—a sphere just 8.9 feet (2.7 m) in diameter and weighing only 705 pounds (320 kg). It was designed to separate from *Cassini* and descend to the surface of Titan, Saturn's huge, mysterious moon. Unlike *Cassini,* which would send information back to Earth for years, *Huygens'* work would be done in less than three hours. During that short time, *Huygens* was to sample Titan's atmosphere, study the energy sources affecting the moon, and take the first up-close look at the surface.

To achieve these goals, *Huygens* was built with a very different set of instruments from *Cassini*'s. The six instruments it carried included special cameras, tools for measuring the density and chemical composition of the atmosphere, an aerosol

This illustration shows the *Huygens* probe detaching from *Cassini* and heading toward Titan (bottom left).

collector for atmospheric particles, and a surface science package designed to help scientists understand the moon's surface. *Huygens* would collect all this material and evidence in a matter of hours and then transmit everything it had learned back to *Cassini*.

In order to achieve this incredibly ambitious goal, *Huygens* would first have to survive the descent to Titan's surface, which scientist had never seen and knew almost nothing about. As scientists on Earth anxiously prepared for the moment when *Huygens* began its part of the mission, they were also busy analyzing the incredible amount of new information they were already receiving from *Cassini.*

Even before entering Saturn's orbit, *Cassini-Huygens* had been adding to what scientists knew about the planet and its moons. A close flyby of the odd little moon called Phoebe showed that it was very different from what had previously been thought. What had seemed a very dark body was actually very bright in places, and it is now believed that Phoebe has a considerable amount of ice.

Not long after its arrival at Saturn, *Cassini-Huygens* discovered three new moons, which were later named Methone, Pallene, and Polydeuces. *Cassini-Huygens* also saw what appeared to be a number of small moons within the planet's rings. Only one of these, now called Daphnis, has been officially recognized. It is the only moon, except for Pan, that is definitely found inside the

Scientists hope that *Cassini*, or some other future Saturn mission, will collect more data to prove that Rhea is the only ringed moon in the Solar System.

rings. *Cassini-Huygens* was not the only observer finding new moons. Astronomers on Earth, often working with new information they had received from the mission, identified at least nineteen small outer moons that were previously unknown. And *Cassini-Huygens* recently found evidence that one of Saturn's major moons, Rhea, may even have a ring system. If this turns out to be true, Rhea will be the only moon in the Solar System known to have its own rings.

ARRIVING AT THE SURFACE OF TITAN

As the end of 2004 approached, scientists, engineers, and technicians managing the *Cassini-Huygens* project were preparing for the most difficult and delicate part of the entire mission. This was the moment when the *Huygens* probe would separate from the *Cassini* orbiter and begin the descent to the surface of Titan.

There was no guarantee that the probe would even survive the trip. Because of the dense clouds of methane, ethane, and other gases shrouding the moon, scientists could only guess what the surface was like. Even before it reached the surface, *Huygens* would be subjected to the intense heat that comes when any object enters an atmosphere at great speed. On December 25, 2004, *Cassini* finally released its probe.

The *Huygens* probe used a series of parachutes to safely descend to Titan's surface.

Twenty-one days later, after a long, slow, gliding approach, *Huygens* began its descent to Titan's surface. During the descent, it constantly sent scientific information to *Cassini*. *Huygens's* descent was slowed by a system of three parachutes that helped to keep it from being destroyed by the heat of atmospheric entry.

The scientists on Earth had to wait a long time to find out whether *Huygens* survived its landing on Titan's surface. The great distance between Titan and Earth meant that transmissions took as long as eighty-five minutes to reach us. But finally, the Deep Space Network, a collection of highly sensitive antennas scattered all over the world, began receiving transmissions relayed by *Cassini.* It was clear that *Huygens* was safe and was

Huygens images like this one may help prove that parts of Titan resemble a young Earth.

now farther from Earth than any other object that had ever landed in space. The first images from *Huygens*'s cameras showed a harsh landscape covered with rocks or chunks of ice. The images and information that *Huygens* sent back in the next few hours changed our view of Titan forever.

We now believe that Titan may actually resemble a young Earth even more closely than was previously believed. Titan may have many of the same features as our planet, including rain, snow, and clouds—most likely made of methane, rather than water— and mountains and valleys. It was once thought likely that methane seas covered much of the planet, but these liquid areas now seem to be concentrated at the moon's poles. Scientists will spend many years analyzing the incredible amounts of information that *Huygens* sent back in such a short time.

Huygens fell silent long ago, its batteries and its instruments dead. However, *Cassini* continues to orbit Saturn. In fact, its mission has proved so successful that it has been extended to include sixty more orbits of the planet. The spacecraft's controllers on Earth plan to keep *Cassini* traveling around Saturn until sometime in 2010. Sometime after that, they will position it in a "safe" orbit around Saturn—where it is unlikely to collide with any of the planet's other satellites—and turn off its instruments.

Multiple images taken by *Cassini-Huygens* in 2004 were put together to create this detailed, natural color view of Saturn and its rings.

FINDING SATURN AT HOME

The *Cassini-Huygens* project—and the *Pioneer* and *Voyager* missions before it—took years of planning, billions of dollars, and some of the most advanced technology ever developed. But it is possible to learn more about Saturn without these kinds of resources. In fact, an amateur astronomer can begin learning about Saturn from his or her own backyard or apartment balcony.

As the ancient astronomers knew, a telescope is not necessary to see Saturn, but it is helpful. Even a relatively weak telescope—one that magnifies objects only thirty times their size—can be used to identify some characteristics of Saturn. This kind of telescope—which is only slightly more powerful than Galileo's early instrument—can allow you to see Titan and Saturn's flattened shape. When a slightly more powerful telescope is used, the A, B, and C rings and the Cassini Division can be seen, as well as several of the other moons.

Whether a telescope is used or not, the most difficult part is finding Saturn as it travels across the sky. The planet appears in the night sky for about nine months of the year. (The rest of the time, it appears above the horizon only in the daytime, when the Sun's bright light makes it difficult or impossible to see.) Unfortunately, for children who want to see Saturn, it is usually most visible in the very early hours of the morning, when they are supposed to be asleep. Saturn is brightest and highest in the sky when it is at **opposition**, which is when the Earth is directly between the Sun and the ringed planet.

During its long, slow orbit around the Sun, Saturn appears in many different areas of the sky. The planet's path changes constantly, so special tools are needed to tell where it can be found at any given time. One of the simplest, most useful, and most inexpensive of these tools is called a **planisphere**. This is a modern version of a device that has been used since ancient times. It consists of two revolving discs, one on top of the other. The bottom disc is a map of the heavens, and the top disc shows the date and time. When the two discs are aligned properly for a particular date and time, the star chart shows where to look to find a celestial object, such as Saturn.

Internet sites and computer software are available that make finding celestial objects as simple as clicking a mouse. Some telescopes even come with their own "star-finding" software built in. And many cities and towns have planetariums or observatories with powerful telescopes that allow people to see breathtaking views of Saturn and the other heavenly bodies. Their programs are among the best ways to learn more about Saturn as our understanding of this fascinating planet changes and grows.

QUICK FACTS ABOUT SATURN

ORIGIN OF NAME: Roman god of agriculture and harvest; Saturn was the father of many other gods.

DISCOVERY: First written mention on Assyrian tablet around 700 BCE; first seen with telescope in 1610 CE

TYPE OF PLANET: Gas giant

DIAMETER AT EQUATOR: 74,900 miles (121,000 km)

DISTANCE FROM SUN: About 839 to 938 million miles (1.3 to 1.5 billion km)

DISTANCE FROM EARTH: 743 million miles (1.19 billion km) to 1 billion miles (1.6 billion km)

LENGTH OF DAY: 10 hours, 32 minutes

LENGTH OF YEAR: Approximately 29.5 Earth years

AVERAGE TEMPERATURE: −300 degrees Fahrenheit (−185 degrees C)

NUMBER OF MOONS: 52 are formally identified and named, but there may be 61 or more

NUMBER OF RINGS: 7 are formally identified and named, but there are thousands

GLOSSARY

asteroid belt—A region in space, between the inner and outer planets, where most asteroids are found.

asteroid—A small body, made mostly of rock, that orbits the Sun.

astronomer—Someone who studies space and the objects in it.

axis—An invisible line around which a celestial object rotates.

celestial—Related to space or the sky.

comet—A small body, made of rock, dust, and ice, that orbits around the sun in a highly elliptical orbit.

constellation—A number of stars that appear from Earth to be grouped together in the sky

dwarf planet—A very small planet with less mass and gravity than other planets.

equator—An invisible line around the middle of a planet, dividing its northern and southern hemispheres.

galaxy—A huge, revolving cluster of stars, gases, and other matter.

gravity—The force between objects that makes them attract each other. The force of gravity increases as objects come closer together and decreases the farther apart they are.

heliocentric—To be Sun-centered. Our Solar System is heliocentric, because the Sun is its center.

light-year—The distance—about 5.9 trillion miles (9.5 trillion km)—that light travels in one year

magnetosphere—The area influenced by a planet's magnetic force.

mantle—An interior section of a planet that is located between the core and the outer crust.

mass—The amount of matter an object contains.

moon—A natural satellite that orbits around a planet

observatory—A place where telescopes and other instruments are used to study space.

opposition—The point where the Earth is directly between the sun and another celestial object.

orbit—To revolve around a celestial object.

physicist—A scientist who studies matter and energy.

planisphere—A device for predicting the movements of celestial objects.

satellite—A celestial object (natural or human-made) that orbits around another body in space.

terrestrial—Relating to land rather than to the sea or atmosphere. Terrestrial planets include Mercury, Venus, Earth, and Mars.

universe—All the matter and energy in existence everywhere

FIND OUT MORE
BOOKS

Barnes-Svarney, Patricia. *A Traveler's Guide to the Solar System*. New York, NY: Sterling Publishing, 2008.

Elkins-Tanton, Linda T. *Jupiter and Saturn*. New York: Chelsea House, 2006.

Goss, Tim. *Saturn*. Chicago: Heinemann Library, 2008.

Graham, Ian. *The Far Planets*. Mankato, MN: Smart Apple Media, 2007.

Howard, Fran. *Saturn*. Edina, MN: ABDO Publishing, 2008.

WEBSITES

Cassini Equinox Mission
http://saturn.jpl.nasa.gov

CoolCosmos: Saturn
http://coolcosmos.ipac.caltech.edu/cosmic_kids/AskKids/saturn.shtml

Find Saturn in the Night Sky
http://saturn.jpl.nasa.gov/kids/activities-nightsky.cfm

NASA Kids' Club
http://www.nasa.gov/audience/forkids/kidsclub/flash/index.html

NASA Solar System Exploration for Kids
http://solarsystem.nasa.gov/kids/index.cfm

NASA Space Place: Saturn
http://spaceplace.nasa.gov/en/kids/cassini_make3.shtml

Saturn
http://www.nineplanets.org/saturn.html

Saturn—Explore the Cosmos
http://www.planetary.org/explore/topics/saturn/

Welcome to the Planets: Saturn
http://pds.jpl.nasa.gov/planets/choices/saturn1.htm

BIBLIOGRAPHY

The author found these resources especially helpful while researching this book.

Aguilar, David. *Planets, Stars, and Galaxies: A Visual Encyclopedia of Our Universe.* Washington, D.C.: National Geographic Society, 2008.

Benton, Julius. *Saturn and How to Observe It (Astronomers' Observing Guides).* London: Springer Science Media, 2008.

Chronicle Online. "Cassini Spacecraft Provides Compelling Evidence for Patterns Resembling Spokes on a Pinwheel in Saturn's Outer Rings." http://www.news.cornell.edu/stories/Nov05/Nicholson.Cassini.lg.html

Frances, Peter. *Universe: The Definitive Visual Guide.* London: Dorling Kindersley, 2006.

Kerrod, Robin. *The Star Guide.* London: Quarto, 2005.

Lovett, Laura, Joan Horvath, and Jeff Cuzzi. *Saturn: A New View.* New York: Abrams, 2006.

NASA: Saturn. http://nssdc.gsfc.nasa.gov/planetary/planets/saturnpage.html

Planet Quest: Exoplanet Exploration. http://planetquest.jpl.nasa.gov/index.cfm

Saturn. http://sse.jpl.nasa.gov/planets/profile.cfm?Object=Saturn

Saturn. http://www.bartleby.com/65/sa/Saturn1.html

University of Tennesse-Knoxville. "The Planet Saturn." http://csep10.phys.utk.edu/astr161/lect/saturn/saturn.html

INDEX

SATURN

ABOUT THE AUTHOR

Terry Allan Hicks has written more than twenty children's books about everything from why people catch colds to how mountains form. He lives in Connecticut with his wife, Nancy, and their three sons, James, Jack, and Andrew.